One Hundred Breaths

Books edited by James P. Roberts

Return To Derleth: Selected Essays

Dark Iowa, Bright Iowa

Return To Derleth: Selected Essays Volume Two

Haunted Voices: Selected Poetry & Art from Lituanus

Love Affairs At The Villa Nelle (with Marilyn L. Taylor)

Books written by James P. Roberts

Derne Runes

Bourland

Famous Wisconsin Authors

Howlin' Wolf!: A Fan's History of the Highs and Lows During Five Stormy Years With the Madison Black Wolf

Spirit Fire

Darkling I Listen, And For Many A Time ... And Other Imaginations

Dancing With Poltergeists

A Demon In My View

Sonnets To Make You Smile

One Hundred Breaths

A collection of poems by
James P. Roberts

Portage Press

Acknowledgements

Some poems were previously published in the following places: *Allegro Poetry Magazine, The Ariel Anthology, Avocet, Bamboo Hut, Blue Heron Review, Bramble, Cacti Fur, Celestial Musings, Echoes, Flutter Poetry Journal, Forage, Foxglove, The Lakefly Writing Contest, Lonesome October Magazine, Madison Green Cab Project, Madison Museum of Contemporary Art, Mirror Dance, Mobius, Red Cedar, Rhythm & Bones: Dark Marrow, Sand Canyon Review, These Fragile Lilacs, The Wisconsin Fellowship of Poets' Calendar, Write Your Madison,* and *Zingara Poetry Review.* "Autumn Burial" was previously published as "Life Of A Leaf." "Fashionable" was previously published as "Lipstick."

The epigraphs come from the following sources:

Bryan Thao Worra, *Tanon Sai Jai*

Lidija Šimkutė, *Tylos Erdvės – Spaces of Silence*

Marina Tsvetayeva, *Selected Poems,* translated by Elaine Feinstein

Joseph Payne Brennan, *Sixty Selected Poems*

Sorrel Mae Florance, *How The Fairies Painted Me*

First printing, 2020

ISBN: 9798642705964

Editor: Morgan Clark

Assistant Editor, Layout, Cover Art: Melanie Hurtgen

To the many cherished Muses
who have inspired these poems to breathe,
may a strong ghost watch over you.

CONTENTS

PROLOGUE

Her stride awakens our stories,

Her smile

Her breath

— Bryan Thao Worra

"A Thousand Smiles"

ONE HUNDRED BREATHS

is how long our kiss lasted
I counted each breath
measuring time against the beat
of your heart

when our lips finally parted
a giant exhalation caught
in my throat I remembered
the taste of warm cherries

such pliable softness
awakened echoes small vibrations
like the ancient songs
of sounding whales

under the sea your body
shifted back to sleep
and I dream now
of one hundred slow breath kisses

hoping when I open my eyes
sunlight will bend fall
across the room
lighting your opening mouth

WHISPERS

Unless we dream

of each other

There will be no mirror

to shine

the image we seek

— Lidija Šimkutė

Tylos Erdvės – Spaces of Silence

THINGS TO REMEMBER

The blizzard of '78
when schools were closed for days
and I had to walk a full mile
to my paper route through
a wind-swept tunnel of snow,
then plod from house to house
delivering newspapers to door,
side porch, mailbox . . .
The young blue-eyed woman,
hair wet from the shower,
she let her towel drop.
Standing in the freezing cold,
her skin a translucent mirror.

ART THOU WOMAN?

Sometimes I see you
find a space
behind the Botticelli.

Reaching out
a divine hand, bony
and spare of thought.

You walk in colors
unknown to the world,
leaving wet footprints.

No one can frame you.
Dressed in gold gilt,
you laugh at fools.

Like the wind,
you breeze through
the dry roads of time.

Like the stars,
you are often distant
from everything.

A CHINESE SILENCE

for Timothy Yu

A young Chinese girl
holds up her father's book of poetry

like a paper shield
dotted with strange words.

Her black eyes shine,
joyfully beseeching people

in the audience to buy the book
Right now!

Before her father has even
finished his recital.

AUTUMN BURIAL

I lay on the brittle grass
beneath the sugar maple
and let falling leaves
cover my face.

I have become
a veined map, replete
with jagged edges
and one long, thin stem.

I smell the scent of earth,
feel soft skin,
my hands at rest,
palms raised toward the sky.

I show my bright colors
for a few days
until the north wind
blows in rain and strips me.

It does not take long
until I am buried.
Sunlight, like an opaque
curtain, blurs my sight.

Frost curls at me
and I have to dig deeper,
knowing all the while
the long months until Spring.

WOMAN, HARP, & TEA

for Kinbria

In the soft glow of light
within the Dobra tea room
I watch her fingers pluck
the strings of her harp.

Aside from the owner,
gazing at empty wicker chairs
and bare tatami mats, I am
the only person in the place
when she begins.

Her dulcet voice brings
visions of lush green pastures
and blazing hearth fires.
The poets of Ireland

stride forth from the past,
their words soaring
in the upper ranges:
echoing lamentations

resound from ancient castle walls
where rugged and lonely coasts
shelter the haunting ghosts
of lost loves, tragic fates.

She nestles her cheek
against the polished frame
like a mother
tending to a sleeping babe.

Outside the window, the street
swarms sweating bodies,
heads down, checking cell phones.
But here, inside the tea room,
it is calm and quiet: the harp,
the singer, and the song
hold me captive
until the clock tolls a closing end.

DIVE-BOMBED

A clap of feathers
and thunder in my ear—

booming squawk
of insistent rage.

A momentary vision
of a black whirlwind
at the corner of my eye.
No warning.

A drone strike pushes me away.

I am surprised,
but understand the primal signal:
Protect the young.

It happened just that once, then
a retreat flight up to the leaf-branched tree
next to the jogging path.

A final clarion breaks the morning's still air
where nothing else moved

but two ducks, floating serenely on the pond.

MY DENTIST'S EYES

Peer into the wide
cavity of my open mouth.
Trapped in this chair, bent back
toward the light, I wonder:
What does she see
beyond the surface decay
brought about by years
of chocolate sweet tooth?
Is she aware that these teeth
she is fixing so perfectly
will be, unless I choose cremation,
the last evidence of my existence?

Some future archaeologist
may uncover me from the dirt,
gauge her handiwork
and call it primitive, then toss
these tiny remnants into a box
to be stored on a dusty shelf.
How fitting a final end!
A day's work by soft hands,
gentle blue eyes
and a wisp of brown hair
(do not forget her smile!)
caught in lamplight.

SOSTENUTO

A long sustained note
Will it rise or will it fall?
ends in a shattered heart.

FASHIONABLE

To get herself ready

                    to write a poem

She puts on lipstick . . .

                    and nothing else

THE LANGUAGE OF STONES

I walk on this land and feel its age.
The oldest rocks in the world lie here,
barely touched by the scourings of time.
Like a fingerprint of forgotten history,
these stones remain in my memory.
I can speak their language—what was
long hidden now revealed as an ancient map.

The menhir—"maen-hir"—long stone
pointing a dread path.
The dolmen with its flat horizontal capstone
like a weighty lid
on all that might have been.
Cromlech: a word so filled with mystery
and fatality it begets visions
of shambling figures wreathed in cold fog,
a procession in search of their kistvaen home,
a dark barrow entrance.
High upon this pixylated tor
I stand and wait for the tumblers to turn.

DISTANCE

Late at night
I walk through the marsh,
far from city lights.
Overhead, the harsh
cry of a hawk.
I stop to look up at the stars,
ignoring a goose's interrupted squawk
and think of how far
distant those pinpoints are
from where I stand,
a tiny speck lost in time,
in a strange land.
Orion's belt,
Cassiopeia's wave,
the box of the Big Dipper:
I felt
infinitesimal, unimportant, save
for a curious and calm acceptance: the world tips
over, seasons change,
years slip past on calendar feet
and I have always been a stranger
passing alone, to a solitary beat.

MARISA LEVITEVA

A name
I imagine:
A tiny bird,
a swallow, perhaps,
rising
into the air,
into the opening sun,
until she
is weightless,
a shadow
against the turning sky.

CRIES

– You and I must have a talk. And

I shiver: let's be brave, shall we?

— Marina Tsvetaeva
Selected Poems

THE EARTHQUAKE PEOPLE

I wander among huddled clots
perched in forlorn, shocked silence.
Piles of rubble loom on all sides.
Somewhere nearby, water flows from a broken
pipe, muddy rivulets soak my feet
clad only in tennis shoes—all I had time to don
apart from a torn black t-shirt and blue jeans—
before the low-roofed house where I'd been staying
collapsed, a rumble I will forever hear no matter
how many days are left. It is the *faces* I look at:
men and women etched in stark colors, these
people of an earthquake land, lives riven
in mere moments. I have never noticed until now
the difference in silences, as if each one has
an assigned weight; the heavier the silence,
the stonier the face I see. Even the dusky babies
cocooned in mother's strong arms have stilled tongues.
I cannot bear the sight—massed thousands dot
the ruined city. Some work, pull at brick mounds,
piece by piece, a conveyor belt of hands free the air
to search for bodies. But quiet, so quiet.
Smoke rises from burning places, trapped beneath
bunched gray clouds with a hint of coming snow.

The silence is broken by a grunt loud as a rifle shot.
More grunts, then a shout, a wave of shouts surge forth.
Heads lift, hands reach to pull from darkness
An infant girl, naked, bloodied, but still alive.

CROSSING BELLS

They signal a warning
That something
Is fast approaching

And you'd better
Get out of the way

For this object
Has a destination

And a time schedule
To meet

If it is to meet
All our growing needs.

The day is bright and sunny
And all there is

In the world

Is that distant sounding

Of what we know
Is coming.

YOUNG WOMAN PEPPER-SPRAYED BY POLICE

How easy it is to force
shouted words back down a hopeful throat
in that space between
the next breath and the scream of pain.
Your gaze narrows to the shiny glare
hiding the face behind the plexi-glass helmet.
Hands deliberately and conspicuously clenched
at your back, there is a man next to you
with right hand raised in a peace sign.

That cloud of spray is now a part of history.
Your name, a goal for the voices of change.
Will you continue to play your part?
Or has the burning led to fearful silence?
Others *will* take up the call, massing in places
where authority holds its iron hand.
This is what we are seeing: the last constriction
of brute assault delivering a virtual meme for the future.

THE JUMPER

He is visible
behind the woman
taking a selfie
with the Golden Gate bridge
in the background.

A tiny dot
like a wounded crow
in the wide space
of blue sky.

The steel spans frame
his descent
while she smiles,
unaware that in the next

second, a geyser will fount,
white ripples widening
to cover the floating body.

DEATH TOLL CLIMBS

what do you say
to a person
who thinks of life

in numbers

and bullets

who measures everything
in buckets of blood

who denies
the charity of others

the forgiveness
so needed

what can you tell them
when there's only
the fuzzy image
cracking their shell

the violence
which is the only language
they now understand

a grave
of flowers

the rising sun

THE SEAMSTRESS MARRIES THE BROKEN MAN

Her life is an opera.
She lives in the costumes she designs.
Every actor is a part of her.

When she met him at a closing night
party, she was attracted
to the indecipherable pain in his eyes.

It wasn't as if she hadn't been warned.
He told her right off who he was, how his life
was so very much different from hers.

He lived in a broken castle. The refrigerator
was broken. The computer was broken.
The TV was not broken, but he only watched

his own collection of movies on the VHS player
(yes, he still had one of those). Everything
about him was broken, except his soul.

That shone out of him like iridescent wings.
That is what she wanted when she married him.
And what she wanted, she usually got.

He came to live with her, eschewing his own
possessions, for the most part, gazing tranquilly
at her exotic pet fish, her vibrant macabre art,

the stylized creations she made and sold on Etsy.
He grew to love her and, inside, he slowly began
to mend what had been thought irreparably broken.

His mind turned into an open book, written
in a language he tried so hard to make her understand.
He laid himself bare to her . . .

In the night of knives, she cut him
into thin slices, strips of flesh sewn into her latest costume.
He did not mind, once he knew her passion.

It was all part of the opera and he still longed
to be there, with her, as the final aria was sung
and the thick curtain, at long last, descended.

THE SEAMSTRESS AND THE GHOST SHROUDS

For as long as she can remember
she has created clothes for ghosts.
Each age poses exquisite challenges
as burial customs change, sometimes
overnight. The easiest shrouds are made
for those who are laid in the ground
bare as the day they were born:
the hardest, the forms of victims
of explosive violence; then, even the ghosts
need to be reconstituted, body parts
brought together as spectres, measured
for appropriate size and texture.

&

Her hands exist in both realms.
Agile, adept, weaving thin white threads
through her ancient changeable loom.
Not all shrouds need to be white.
But she will not use black thread:
To do so invites the wearer to a doom
far greater than ever imagined.
For Mardi Gras, Kwanzaa, Cinco De Mayo
or other cultural festivals, the shrouds
explode in luminous colors. At night,
the cemetery morphs into a riotous bacchanal.
Ghosts have always known how to dance.

&

She has had many lovers—both male
and female: when they die, she takes the utmost
care with their shrouds. This way some part
of them still lives, still aware, still wanting
her haunting embrace, her tenuous cloth,
her nebular lips: the kiss of a pristine death
remembered. As there will always be ghosts
eventually wandering to her door, the seamstress
continues to work, crafting her own surprising shroud.

FLOW POETRY IN HUE, VIETNAM

for Adam

You speak to your ancestors
lying in shallow graves
mulched over by jungle.

You speak to alligators
and elephants, native creatures
who remember much.

You speak to huddled mothers
of black-eyed babies who utter
never a word or cry.

You speak to bamboo winds,
hollow temples, dynasties fallen
and long forgotten.

You speak to fog-shrouded mountains,
roiling, chocolate Mekong River,
a black market dog tag.

You speak to rows of mildewed books
in a dozen languages—histories
yearning to be heard.

The raucous birds speak to you:
Go back home or we will use your dreads
to feather our lonely nests.

ROLLER DERBY

for Mouse

Tonight she feels it, the tug of gravity as she whirls
around the track counterclockwise. The pack looms
ahead, bodies shift to squish together, trying to block her.
But she sees a tiny crack and, tiny herself, with a burst
almost too fast to follow, darts through and scores
more points. The crowd erupts, calling her derby name
like the honking of geese < > A decade now, she's skated
with these women, who come and go, kindred spirits
for a season or two, but she has returned, year after year,
her thick twin braids a recognizable trademark. How long
she will continue, she does not know, only that she still
relishes the thrill of speeding along to the energy
of the crowd, the pulse of her heart, the rumble of the skates
and all the mad happiness she can contain.

CONSTELLATION YOGA

Three women
dressed in leotards
and sitting on blankets,
begin their forms.

They make a perfect triangle
with legs crossed
and hands resting on bony knees,
palms up.

When they lay down
on their backs
and raise their legs,
I see
Orion's belt
and know that
an arrow has been loosed.

One calls herself
a "Pescatarian,"
stretching forward
to touch
her painted toes.

A fish jumps
near the shore
and the talk
turns to tacos,
hot and heavy
like Venus
in transit.

But now
the women cluster
thick as the swarm
of the Pleiades seen
through a telescope.

I hear
suppressed grunts
as they solemnly rise,
hands thrust to the sky
following Andromeda's
wavy lines.

Plummet now to Earth,
hands and knees clutch grass,
taut backs hump toward
Ursa Minor.

Supple thighs crease
as growling stomachs
inhale breath,
exhale molecules.

The session concludes,
blankets are folded
and in the dark
firefly-lit night,
a soft voice intones
"Same time, next week."

"Let's do the Big Dipper!"

B. B. KING AND THE BIG DOGS BLUES

The big dogs bark when B. B. King
walks by their chains and fences
because dogs can recognize someone
who howls the blues in the night
at the round white moon
better than they ever will.

That old black strap guitar
shining in the gaudy bar lights
reflects the pain in his
wandering eyes. Each drawn-out note
brings memories of bad masters with rolled-up
newspaper in hand, ready to strike.

Today, unexpectedly, my life turned
into a big dog's dish.
People I once loved now fighting
over worthless, pitiful scraps, without dignity.
B. B. King has known, has walked
that side of the street.

Sometimes, I watch the big dogs
as they sleep and dream, paws twitching
in reflex, ears erect to catch the sound of a hurt.
On the stereo, B. B. King plays his final
bluesy song, melding the world
into six silver strings.

BRING ME THE HEAD OF A FALLEN GOD

(Federico Castellon: *Dream On The Beach*)

See the empty eyes where all knowledge has been plucked out,
now lost. We have abandoned the ideals of an age, the laurels
of heroism rendered meaningless. No wonder our emaciated bodies
show skeletal, even though we continue to primp and pose
before narcissistic mirrors. Yet some stand naked, transfixed
beneath the arch of a red solar giant future, while others slump,
hand over face, unwilling to look at what we have wrought.
Pitiless desert sands, a ravaged planet: this is our existence today.
The golden tongue cut out, the voice of reason silenced.
We dine on the scraps of desiccated desire.
Our blood runs dry, we have become marble.

FIELD GUIDE TO THE PERSEIDS

To see the Perseids
one must stay up late
and travel away from the light
into August's starry night.

A place where the horizon
is clear, free of obstructed
viewing: the countryside
works well, although

it is hard to find an area
apart from a city's distant
glow. It is best to see
the Perseids alone

or with one other person.
Some treasured kindred soul
to share this experience
of listening to messages

from the cosmos. Indeed,
there *is* a sound, a whispery
buzz as rocks enter
and burn up in the atmosphere.
(Voices of the Gods)

Tonight, I am with you
as we lay entwined
on a blanket, looking up.

Here they come, flashing
brilliance lasting but the moment
of a heartbeat. I take your hand.

DOLMEN WITCH

She lives among the old stones
pocking this barren rocky land.
Small tufts of grass grow
between moss-filled cracks.

During the day she wanders
down to the shore
of the gray sea to collect
what has been thrown away.

Her dark dress and fringed shawl
stand silhouette
in the early dawn light
while gulls screech overhead.

She has been with us, always.
She is known, even to the eldest
who say she is the same now
as when they were stripling youths.

When night falls
and a full moon rises,
she dances sky-clad
to a faint sound of pipes.

Thirteen rabbits form a circle
to caper around her.
Mist blooms from the rocks.
Shadows begin to move.

SHOUTS

We will tremble and creep down the stair;

we will slide down the street and dance on the stones,

wearing a ratskin coat on our castanet bones.

— Joseph Payne Brennan

"The Dancer"

ICE

to them it must seem like
donning a second skin

bullet proof
bomb proof

heavy with authority

impervious to the ocean
of bare skin behind wire cages

inured to haunted eyes
having escaped one suffering

only to find themselves
trapped in another

a revolving door
ready to eject them
back to the bloody hunt

but those officers
must put away their inborn guilt

scrape it free
from their own skin

hang it by a legal hook

step back
and do it all over

again

MURDERSQUISHING

You swarm about me.
The heat rises
until it is two degrees
over the limit
of endurance.

I feel as if I am in a ball,
the eye of a cyclone
where air pressure is so low,
breathing is hard as ice.

You are a Japanese hornet,
scary and voracious, able to rip
forty of me into tasty pieces
in less than a minute.

This is called murdersquishing:
The bees against the hornet.
I call it one hell of a night
with you in our hive-sized bed.

I am your honey bee,
often defenseless, a male drone
servicing my regal queen
only to wobble drunkenly away to die,
my purpose achieved.
Sometimes, murder is not so bad.

ROOM OF DOLLS

It scares me
to be
in a silent room
full of dolls.

Dark doors
close me in.

I see

rows of glassy eyes
and the same
set smiles,
carefully styled hair,
in period dresses.

Arranged
just so artfully.

What fell thoughts
accrue
in night's quiet air?

What hidden knives
pursue?

What tread upon the floor?

Abandoned love
come for revenge.

WHITE NOSE

We got it from the bats.
Tiny teeth sinking into our veins,
microscopic microbes
abandoning one dying carrier
and entering another.

It spread rapidly, any liquid secretion
to touch skin brought forth
unmistakable symptoms.
Our noses flattened and turned up.
Our sight began to dim, seeing only shadows.

Hearing, however, improved to the point
where mobility was directed by sonar
rather than sight, our ears turned triangular.
Most disturbing of all:
This sudden craving for fresh blood.

The flesh beneath our arms expanded.
Our young soon learned to fly.
The old human shapes eventually died out.
Tonight, we will celebrate our evolution
beneath the white glow from the old moon.

We will hibernate when winter comes.

TWO WOMEN IN A YURT, AFTER THE QUAKE

for Dr. Jatinda Cheema

It is eerie, the silence that follows once the ground has finally settled.
Displaced rocks roll to a stop and the trees slowly subside their
      almost musical sway.
Startled birds nervously resume their plaintive song. *It is over now.*
      We are still here.

Outside the yurt standing alone on the level plain, Mongush
has calmed the skittish horse while young Sadip looks on in aloof
      disdain,
arms folded across his thin chest. Both are wearing their winter garb:
      a bearskin
Malgai with ear flaps, a thick *nekhii* parka, leather trousers and
      knee-high boots.

In the distance, snow-covered mountains sprawl beneath a blue sky
scattered with puffs of fleecy white clouds which merge with plumes
      of snow
blowing off the highest peaks. The baby girl, Samyan, cries loudly in
      her wooden crib.

The yurt is undamaged. A teardrop-shaped four-string *tovshuur*
      hanging
on a peg wall remains intact. The inner rim of the yurt roof is
      decorated
with bright orange and blue designs, a parade of mandalas
      circumscribing good fortune.
A prayer wheel spins unceasingly and intricately patterned
      rugs carpet the yurt floor.

Two women stand ground in the middle of the yurt. The younger
        woman, Namesh, hides
in the background while her mother, Suunyu, gazes steadily
        forward, her seamed face hard
as granite. It is evident there has been a quarrel, still not ended, only
        delayed
by the earthquake. It will resume once the men have departed.

This is a land of earthquakes: voices of gods. An old land where
        mountains loom
to dizzying heights, then fall steeply to be swallowed in trackless
        deserts. Stories
live here, told at night to the smoke of burning yak butter candles.
One looks up and feels the immensity of stars, blazing like the
        pitiless eyes of angry deities.

The women are cautious, rife with knowledge handed down through
        generations
of the fragile relationship of things. Centuries of secrets form in their
        eyes and worn faces.
Beneath the traditional dresses they wear are hard bodies sculpted
        by wind, sun, and toil.
Strong, ridged hands create tools, cook day and night, hold crying
        babies.

There women even an earthquake cannot destroy, they simply
        endure.

JESUS PORTRAIT

on the floor
i spread my arms wide
ready to be crucified

fire on my fingertips
a holy hole in my mouth

clouds roll by outside
indifferent   denied
forming & re-forming whips

bloodying truth

cumulonimbus energy
passing up gone souls

heaven's stormy synergy
air heavy as biblical books

i blink & see neutrinos
rivering two directions
everywhere i look

now comes nails   hands

again

blood

in a moment i also
will be risen

above the raging flood
seeking flight   redemption

LITHUANIA: SEASHORE DREAM

for Lidija Šimkutė

She stands at the cusp of the Baltic
high cheekbones
taut with passion, memories.

She holds amber in her hands,
draws a stone blade across her neck,
cuts her hair to feed the tides.

She is a language of rain,
dark forests and sunsets.
At night, the wolves howl.

My stumbling mouth
spumes soft sibilants
ending in *-us*: you and I.

My embrace eludes capture.
She flits away,
A pale ghost of history.

She leaves behind a memento:
pages of the past
written on the skin of my body.

HAUNTING EYES

for Hildegarde Neff

She stares directly at the camera
as if she is able to read all the secrets
hidden behind the lens.

Her large blue eyes are so wide
they invite the dizzying plummet,
drawn irresistibly into her presence.

Those eyes have captured memories,
held them like fragile, broken children.
Memories so dark, they bleed black.

The war, the Soviet prison camp, the escape:
All the thousand of witnessed dead,
brought to life once more in film.

An actress, she learned to use her rolling, poison eyes
and her frail, often ill, body as testament:
You still cannot see who I am.

A sinner, her nakedness exposed to the world.
A survivor of the Hollywood holocaust.
A woman who looked at the gift horse—and wept.

YEVGENY

You have gone on
to see the face behind the face .

A place where words
come to you so easily
there is no longer the need to speak.

I remember that night
in April 2001 when you came to Madison,
reciting poems in English
and Russian to a crowded auditorium.

What struck me most
was the mobility of your face:
a Lon Chaney Jr. of poets,
able to wear any disguise

you chose.
          But it was the tired,
wrinkled, generous smile. A smile
I sometimes think only poets
can find.
          It had that luminosity
One discovers in the paintings of saints.

I always thought your name
sounded like the rapids of a river,
rushing through a narrow canyon
to spill out into the round O of a lake.

Tonight, I look at the stars in the sky,
whispering your poem to the rising mist.

WOMAN ON A BENCH WHO COULD NOT SMILE

She gazes intently at her companion,
long brown hair framing a Cassandra face.
Her stark, stricken expression reveals
she is hearing bad news,
patiently holding herself inside.

She clearly wants to help, but silence here
is the most comfort she can offer.
There is no room on this gray, blustery day
for a smile. The other woman is short,
squat, wearing dark glasses behind which
you know there are purple-black bruises.

The slump of her shoulders shout defeat
and her straight black hair lies limp, unstirred
by the wind. A steady stream of people
hurry by, eyes averted, detouring around
their island of solitude. Bicyclists flash past,
there and gone, but the women stay focused.

Finally, the unsmiling woman with the pain
in her eyes, rises, pulling her friend up into an embrace.
After some moments, they reluctantly release, apart,
but still holding firm hands. As one, the two women
turn and disappear into the crowd, leaving behind
a now empty bench.

LAMENTS

Where emerald wisdoms spring forth

gushing the ancient stories,

where my reflection doesn't matter anymore

—Sorrel Mae Florance

"Reflections In A Mirror"

WHY CAN'T I REMEMBER THE STARTING LINEUP
OF THE 1944 ST. LOUIS BROWNS?

I used to know them
like my breakfast cereal.
Gaunt faces, hollow eyes,
baggy uniforms, sweat-stained caps
and tobacco chew bulging their cheeks.

They slept with me at night,
chasing fly balls in my dreams.
Ghostly figures from cardboard
squares, collected in shoeboxes
and clipped from yellowed newspapers.

Doomed to failure, always compared to their
crosstown Cardinal cousins — to think
they once had Branch Rickey! — save for one
magical war-time season when all the best
players were gone. These stone-jawed
former miners, farmers, itinerant bush-leaguers
and one-armed draft rejects won an improbable
pennant! Their names are graven in history.

Ah! But time has worn them thin.
Faded scraps of a dim and distant year.
I can no longer count on lunch money
won on a bet that I could name
the starting lineup of the 1944 St. Louis Browns
or the 1955 Brooklyn Dodgers, or even
those perennial white elephants, the Philadelphia Athletics.

The ball disappears over the fence,
beyond my frantically waving Vern Stephens autographed glove.

BASEBALL

It's been years
ball   bat
spin
as heavy
as dreams of a
young boy
chasing his own
afternoon shadow
across summer's long dry brittle grass
across his father's deep-held belief

that nothing he can do
will change this boy into a man
Nevertheless
a love of sound   boom
of a crowd's disruptive
clamor echoing birds from
dusty rafters now following its trajectory all
the way out
into the sun's deep space
So much tradition
Bound up in one whirlwind fatal instant

O boy contemplating suicide today
It all depends now on
whether or not you
can catch up to that
descending white sphere your still growing athletic body
clad in whitest cloth
cross bearing

symptoms of what might have
occurred had you not got a

late jump start

running   running
fast
faster   fastest   you
O give me back that moment when ball met bat
for I am not ready
to meet truth
It is there before your stark face
Your hand grips
clenches and then unclenches
the heart

MOTHER PLANET

They keep coming, relentless,
despite my best efforts to get them to stop.

Systems failures, crash landings, inhospitable
atmospheres—a great loss of life.

But every year sees a sleek new ship
pointing like an arrow at my surface

ready to plunge into my center
and reveal all my hidden secrets.

I understand their urgency,
their own planet

is nearly at its burnt-out core
while I have billions of years left.

It's hard for me to leave my womb
just to clean up their ungodly mess

once the pieces have stopped dividing
in some weird parthenogenetic symbiosis.

But I persist—and have for far more revolutions
of my gas giant sun than I am remembering.

I go backwards sometimes, fated to see
re-enactments of event horizons already known.

The only pleasure I get is the shocked look
behind their glassine masks when they discover

the welcome I have painstakingly set out: rows
of their own bodies,

clean and sharp, the exoskeletal spacesuits
as pristine as the distant stars.

UPON READING LYN LIFSHIN'S *KISS THE SKIN OFF*

small eggs
hatch
small poems

*

trying to find
a word to fit
into the poem

three more scurry away

*

writing a poem
is like fencing
parry, riposte, thrust

a little blood spilt
as the tongue dries

*

i wish i could find
a mad girl
i could turn
into a poem

*

when you dont know
her name

she makes one
says its just
for you

*

too many women
at your poetry
reading
not enough poems
to go around

*

when you got lost
in Madison

i wrote a poem
to bring you out

*

Robin Hood
never wrote
poetry

all my arrows
stuck in you

quivering

MIDNIGHT CURATOR OF THE LITTLE FREE LIBRARIES

I call them my children,
these repositories of the last read.

Little boxes of books
like fields of colorful poppies

all around the city of lakes.
In them, I search for the old,

the out-of-place, the curiously strange
in hopes of a future revelation.

At midnight I make my rounds,
for that is when the books come alive.

I hear them speak in that language
which lies beyond the printed page.

One or two, I take home,
new orphans of the technological war.

The remainders are straightened properly,
arranged like obedient soldiers.

I close the wobbly door and leave
the Little Free Library standing

by itself in the space between shadows,
a sentinel in the moonlight.

MOON LUTE

The wood is aged Qing Dynasty,
before the rise of industrial China.
Horsehair braided strings,
sharply plucked, sing dulcet tones.
The bridge is a crescent-shaped
piece of stone pine . . . what a trial
to thread those tiny holes
so irregularly spaced!

Symbols of dragon and phoenix
entwined in mutual fire.
The wooden pegs squeak
as you twist tighter
until they are at the edge of snapping.
The music in this delicate instrument
has been trapped for centuries.
You set it free in dips of bone stroke,
scented lotus, a waiting body.

Two ancient birds share the same dream.

QUARTER REST

Your body throbs,
pulses in time to heartbeats.
Eyes dark as treble clefs
in a D minor dirge, diadems
of tears glisten in soft light.
Fingernails scratch pizzicato
on my shoulder blades, stretched
toward heaven, *oh apassionata!*
Bass line heavy with portent
weaves through sweat-soaked sheets,
wraps itself around a thick stalk,
squeezes out a motet. Lost
amidst night's music, I rest
in fourths, arms and legs divided
to find a symphonic voice
uttering the divine.

LIFTING A SUNBEAM

When you have spent all your life
in darkness
the thickness of a sunbeam
slowly creeping across the floor
can be as heavy
as Atlas shouldering the world
or as light as the pages
of a book of dreams.

FIGS

I crave figs.
Their brown sweetness reminds me
of love.

I chew love, roll it
on my tongue, savor the rising juice.

Pluck me a fig, o nymph!
Dangle it before my lips.

Taunt me with the color
of your hair as it brushes
my brow.

Heart, you are a fig
from which I have removed

the leaf.

YOUR BOOK

As we lay in bed
I want to hear
all the stories
you have not yet told me.
My mind
is an open blank book
needing to be filled.
Your tongue
will write the pages
one by one
but I know
with great, great sorrow
if you choose
your stories
your book
can always and only
be yours.

ETERNITY

All night long in Isfahan
we spoke around the shadows
of minarets and drank our
lemon tea and ate glazed *kebabs*,
knowing that tomorrow
would bring crowds of believers
toting Qurans and Uzis
in equal proportions, the fires
of paradise in their black sun-burnt
desert eyes, hearts locked
in bullets of steel.

A nightingale cried out, thirsting
for our sweet *jerez* nightcap,
pecking at faded mosaics—
still reflections of similar birds.
Full yellow moon poured down
Arabic benedictions, tiny stars
explode, raining stones
on the tumbling world.
All the while, our repentant gaze
fused together
in foreigners' prayer, seeking
fragrant dreams,
an unending garden.

ELEGY FOR WOO WOO

life

you give me
this cup

full of sorrow

I drink

taste its sharp
bitter tang

every year
another cup

I drink

I do not thirst
yet

you keep giving
me more

until the tears
finally flow

add vinegar
to this wound

this torn heart

But she . . . ?
A ghost, a revenant
but lately
resurrected

only to be
shriven

into
your parting embrace?

Still
I drink

will continue
to drink

even
when you present me

with dry hands
that last cup

her last word

sleep

EPILOGUE

Now we see indistinctly, as in a mirror;

then we shall see face to face.

—1 Corinthians 13:12

THE STATIONS OF THE POET: A PILGRIMAGE
OCTOBER 31, 2010, INDIAN LAKE COUNTY PARK

For my mother, Cyrilla Roberts (1926-2010)

I : ARRIVAL

Frost from a cold, starry night coats the grass
as I enter the paved lot and park facing north. Silence,
suddenly broken by geese honking in flight overhead,
the sky stirred with pale wisps of cirrus clouds.
Last night's revelry a memory: I have a purpose
on *this* morning, the final day of October.
A month of Fall.

II : THE STAFF

I take my hiking stick, companion
of many adventures, now shiny and worn
with a great crack split partway down its middle.
Knobby protrusions caress my soft hands.
It becomes my Cross today. I carry it proudly,
Unbent, undaunted, determined to take
the path I must follow.

III : LAKE OF SORROW

Leaves scuttle in a light wind, a far cry
from the storms earlier in the week.
Their softness masks my journey
down the rock-strewn trail beside the lake
whose still waters reflect blue heavens.
Pussywillows flank me as I pause to remember
that acute pain: the finality of loss.

IV: SIGNS

At the crest of a rise there is a commemorative bench
and a sign: a poem by Tennessee Williams
where one walks the grasses of heaven, barefoot.
I look out over grass, to distant farms, at the rolls
of hay dotting the land. A glint of sunlight on windows.
It is a serene panorama. I feel the heaviness in my heart
slide away, vanishing into the browning grass.

V : MT. CALVARY

Once I could *run* up this steep incline
in those days when I ran through *everything*.
Today, sharp-edged rocks pierce my feet,
I stumble over twisted roots,
my breath loud as a 1913 steam locomotive.
A woodpecker drums news of my progress.
A fallen tree log beckons. I sink down and rest.

VI : PERILOUS WOODS

A sprig of tiny red berries, tempting surcease,
like an apple. Thick bare trees close in, branches
clack and appear to grasp the dying breath of summer.
Other penitents now pass by, hurrying toward needs,
desires, disappointments. Two more poems loom ahead:
Sara Teasdale's "May Day" and I think of one
who will never see May again. W. H. Davies speaks
of "Leisure." I take my time and stare somnolently
at leaves, at trees, at sepia-tinted sun.

VII : MEADOW OASIS

One logy dragonfly wearily hovers amidst dry weeds,
a late season holdover, wings dusty with age. Woodpecker
rattle has followed me here to this wooden bench
at the meadow's edge. A blue jay screeches defiance
and flits from tree branch to weedy ground.
A hollow walnut tree sports a round hole where I imagine
sleepy owl eyes watch: *do they see her presence?*

VIII : GOLGOTHA

I climb gravel steps which embark on a narrow path
ending at a wooden stairway: a strait gate of 86 paces,
each taken with agony on a bad ankle: I have gone too far,
I cannot turn back. Behind me is a cabin where I briefly stopped
to wash my face from sweat—the cloth retains the imprint.
Now I pass through a copse of white crosses: paper birches
standing sentinel, arms flung over wide spaces.

IX : THE CHAPEL

I have written of it before: built in 1852.
A place for private devotions of yesteryear.
I open the gate, leaving my stick outside.
At the door I enter, ducking under the low doorframe
and kneel before the statue of the Virgin. I take out
the candle from my mother's bedroom and light it.
A Bible rests before me, so I turn the pages, reading,
praying, remembering the One who bore me here.

X : RESURRECTION

I am the gnarled old oak I sit beneath, as the sun
lowers over the valley. My roots are now here,
in Wisconsin. The past is gone, only shades remain.
A yearly tradition diminishes, no more trips to my child-
hood home, my former self cast adrift, transfigured.
I rise with my Cross and descend the steps back
to where I had begun, shedding what I once was
to be born anew, in a new sun.